About Me: Chris T. Risen

Hello and welcome! I'm Chris T. Risen, a seasoned professional with an extensive background in direct marketing, affiliate marketing, sales funnels, and leading dynamic sales teams. With years of invaluable experience under my belt, I've had the privilege of being a partner in one of the esteemed organizations recognized on the Inc 500 list of fastest-growing companies.

Professional Background

My journey in the dynamic field of marketing began over a decade ago, where my innate passion for connecting products with people found its true calling. Over the years, I have dedicated my skills and effort to marketing, where I've worked tirelessly to understand the intricacies and nuances that drive successful campaigns.

I've spearheaded marketing initiatives for eight distinctive brands, each with its unique identity, audience, and market position. This diversity in experience has not only broadened my perspective but also deepened my insights into the multifaceted world of marketing, making me adaptable and proficient in handling various marketing challenges and opportunities.

Expertise

Direct Marketing: With a robust background in direct marketing, I've developed and executed campaigns that directly engage the target audience, driving response and conversions through carefully crafted strategies and messages.

Affiliate Marketing: In the realm of affiliate marketing, I've worked on both sides of the spectrum—promoting products as an affiliate and driving sales through affiliates. This comprehensive experience has provided me with a deep understanding of the affiliate marketing landscape.

Sales Funnels: Mastering the art and science of sales funnels, I've successfully created and optimized conversion-focused funnels that not only attract but also retain customers, maximizing lifetime value and enhancing customer satisfaction.

Sales Teams: Leading high-performance sales teams has been one of my areas of expertise. By fostering a collaborative and motivated environment, I've guided teams to exceed sales targets while maintaining a focus on providing value to our clients and customers.

Inc 500 Fastest Growing Company Partnership: Being a partner in an Inc 500 recognized company has been a monumental milestone in my career. It is a testament to the collective hard work, innovation, and relentless pursuit of excellence that defines my approach to business and marketing.

My Approach

I approach marketing as a dynamic, evolving field that requires a blend of creativity, analytics, and an unerring focus on customer needs. In every campaign, strategy, or project I undertake, the customer is always at the core. By understanding their needs, preferences, and behaviors, I craft marketing strategies that resonate, engage, and convert.

Here's to successful marketing endeavors and the exciting journey that each campaign brings. Looking forward to crossing paths with like-minded professionals, collaborators, and enthusiasts in the field!

Chris T. Risen

Introduction

Brief Overview

Welcome to "A Beginner's Guide to Real Estate Investing: Passive Income Made Simple" - your stepping stone into the engaging world of real estate investment! This book is designed to usher you into a domain where financial freedom and long-term wealth are not only possible but very achievable through strategic and informed investment decisions.

Real estate investment, at its core, involves purchasing, managing, and selling real estate properties with the primary objective of generating income and securing long-term financial gains. This sector presents an array of opportunities for both novice and seasoned investors, making it a preferred choice for individuals seeking to create a sustainable source of passive income. Whether you envision owning a small rental property or a series of commercial buildings, this book will guide you through the necessary steps to turn these visions into tangible reality.

Purpose of the Book

The primary aim of this guide is to demystify the process of real estate investing for beginners. Starting your journey in real estate investment can often feel daunting due to the sheer volume of information and the perceived complexities of the market dynamics. This guide seeks to simplify this process, providing you with the foundational knowledge and tools necessary to navigate the real estate market confidently.

The chapters ahead will unfold the various types of real estate investments available, elucidating the characteristics, benefits, and challenges of each. We will delve into the financing options accessible to you as an investor, guiding you through the procedures of selecting, acquiring, and managing your investment properties. Furthermore, the book will highlight common pitfalls and mistakes to avoid, offering invaluable insights and tips garnered from seasoned investors and industry experts.

Through "A Beginner's Guide to Real Estate Investing", our mission is to empower you with the knowledge and confidence to make informed investment decisions that align with your financial goals and aspirations. Whether you are taking the initial steps towards financial independence or seeking to diversify your investment portfolio, this guide is crafted with your needs in mind, providing practical, actionable insights to steer you towards success in the vibrant world of real estate investing. Embark on this enlightening journey with us, and uncover the potentials and rewards that real estate investing generously offers!

Chapter 1: Understanding Real Estate Investing

Definition

Real estate investing can be succinctly defined as the act of purchasing, owning, managing, leasing, or selling real estate properties with the intent of earning a profit. Unlike buying a home for personal use, real estate investing focuses on the generation of income or capital appreciation. The property acquired can either serve as a long-term asset, regularly producing rental income, or be sold after its value appreciates over time.

Types of Real Estate Investing

The realm of real estate is vast, offering a myriad of investment opportunities. Here are some of the most prominent types:

1. **Residential Real Estate:** This involves investing in homes, apartments, townhouses, and vacation houses. Investors earn through rental income, typically on a monthly basis. The lease agreements often last a year, depending on the preference of the tenant and landlord.
2. **Commercial Real Estate:** This pertains to properties used for business purposes. Examples include office buildings, warehouses, and retail spaces. These leases often span a longer duration than residential ones, ensuring a more extended, consistent income stream for investors.
3. **Industrial Real Estate:** Encompassing properties like factories, warehouses, and industrial sheds, these investments offer income through both rent and potential production output.
4. **Retail Real Estate:** Shopping centers, malls, and any other retail storefronts fall under this category. Investors might earn from the rent and sometimes a percentage of the business's sales, a concept known as percentage rent.
5. **Raw Land:** This involves purchasing vacant land with

the prospect of selling it to developers or using it for development purposes.

6. **Real Estate Investment Trusts (REITs):** These are companies that own or finance income-producing real estate across various sectors. Investing in REITs is akin to investing in stocks, providing a way to invest in real estate without purchasing physical property.

Benefits and Risks

As with any investment opportunity, real estate comes with its unique set of benefits and risks.

Benefits:

- **Passive Income Generation:** Once set up correctly, real estate can provide a consistent and passive income stream, especially through rental properties.
- **Capital Appreciation:** Over time, the value of real estate properties generally appreciates, leading to increased net worth for investors.
- **Tax Benefits:** Real estate investors often enjoy tax deductions on property taxes, mortgage interest, and depreciation.
- **Diversification:** Real estate can be a great way to diversify an investment portfolio, reducing the overall risk.
- **Leverage:** Real estate allows investors to buy properties with a small down payment and use the property itself as collateral to secure financing for the rest.

Risks:

- **Market Volatility:** Real estate markets can be cyclical, with periods of rapid appreciation followed by stagnation or even depreciation.
- **High Entry Costs:** The initial capital required for real estate can be high, especially when compared to other forms of investment.
- **Management Challenges:** Properties require regular maintenance, and dealing with tenants can sometimes be

challenging.
- **Liquidity Issues:** Unlike stocks or bonds, real estate is not easily convertible to cash. Selling a property can be a long process.
- **Interest Rate Sensitivity:** If financed with a mortgage, the cost of investment can rise if interest rates increase.

Conclusion

Real estate investing is a multifaceted domain offering various opportunities for profit. Like any venture, it comes with its challenges, but with thorough research, proper planning, and continuous learning, it can serve as a rewarding avenue towards financial growth and stability.

Chapter 2: The Concept Of Passive Income

What Is Passive Income?

At its core, passive income is money earned with minimal to no active effort. It contrasts sharply with active income, where one is directly trading time for money, such as wages earned from a job. Passive income is often associated with investments or ventures that require an initial effort or capital outlay but subsequently operate with little daily involvement from the investor. This doesn't mean that passive income requires no work; rather, the bulk of the work is upfront, and the revenue generated afterward is more hands-off.

Examples of passive income include dividends from stocks, royalties from intellectual properties, and, most pertinent to our discussion, rental income from real estate properties.

Importance of Passive Income

- **Financial Security:** Passive income streams can provide added financial security, supplementing active incomes and serving as a cushion during economic downturns or personal financial challenges.
- **Wealth Accumulation:** Over time, consistent passive income can lead to significant wealth accumulation, especially if reinvested.
- **Financial Independence:** For many, the ultimate goal of generating passive income is achieving financial independence, where one's passive income meets or exceeds their living expenses. This allows for greater choices in life, from pursuing passions without financial pressures to early retirement.
- **Leveraged Time:** By decoupling time from income, passive income grants individuals more free time. This time can be used for leisure, further investment opportunities, or other

pursuits.

- **Reduced Financial Stress:** With a steady stream of passive income, financial uncertainties and stresses are significantly reduced, leading to a better quality of life.

Passive Income and Real Estate

Real estate stands out as one of the most popular and effective vehicles for generating passive income. Here's how:

- **Rental Properties:** After the initial effort of acquiring a property and finding tenants, landlords can earn a consistent income from rent. While there are responsibilities like property maintenance and tenant management, much of the daily oversight can be handed off to property management companies, further enhancing the "passiveness" of this income.
- **Real Estate Investment Trusts (REITs):** By investing in REITs, individuals can earn a share of the income generated from real estate properties without actually owning them. This income is usually in the form of dividends, making it a truly passive investment.
- **Seller Financing:** In cases where an investor sells a property and offers financing to the buyer, the investor can earn passive income from the interest on the financed amount.
- **Real Estate Partnerships: If** one party provides the capital while another handles property acquisition and management, passive income can be generated for the silent partner, who isn't actively involved in day-to-day operations.

Conclusion

In essence, real estate offers a plethora of avenues for generating passive income. With the right strategies, informed decisions, and initial diligence, real estate can become a cornerstone in an individual's passive income portfolio, bringing them closer to financial independence and a life of greater choice and freedom.

Chapter 3: Getting Started With Real Estate Investing

Initial Capital

Getting started in real estate investing invariably requires some degree of initial capital. This capital is utilized to purchase your first property, cover closing costs, and meet other related expenses.

1. **Savings:** The simplest way to accumulate initial capital is through savings. Set aside a certain percentage of your income regularly until you amass enough to make your first investment.
2. **Loans and Mortgages:** Various financial institutions offer loans and mortgages tailored for real estate investments. You might need a solid credit score and a stable income source to qualify for these loans.
3. **Partnerships:** Engaging in partnerships can significantly lower individual capital requirements. In such arrangements, partners contribute funds, and in some cases, different expertise to the venture.
4. Investment Groups: Joining real estate investment groups allows individuals to invest in rental properties without having to manage them, making it a suitable option for those with limited capital.

Before proceeding, it's crucial to understand your financial position, risk tolerance, and investment goals. Also, consider consulting with a financial advisor or real estate expert for personalized advice.

Real Estate Research

Thorough research is pivotal in mitigating risks associated with real estate investing.

1. **Market Analysis:** Understand the current state of the real estate market. Identify areas with high growth potential and study market trends, as these will influence property values and rental income.
2. **Location:** Location significantly impacts property value. Research neighborhoods, considering factors like safety, amenities, schools, and future development plans in the area.
3. **Property Type:** Decide the type of property you want to invest in, considering your budget and investment goals. Each property type comes with distinct advantages, challenges, and management requirements.
4. **Financial Analysis:** Perform a meticulous financial analysis, calculating potential costs, expected returns, cash flow, and return on investment (ROI).

Forming an Investment Strategy

Developing a clear investment strategy is fundamental to your success in real estate investing.

1. **Define Objectives:** Clearly articulate your investment goals, whether it's generating passive income, property appreciation, or a combination of both.
2. **Investment Horizon:** Determine your investment horizon, understanding that real estate is typically a long-term venture.
3. **Risk Management:** Develop a risk management plan, considering factors like market volatility, interest rates, and economic downturns.
4. **Diversification:** Consider diversifying your investments across different property types and locations to spread risk.
5. **Continuous Learning:** Stay informed about the real estate market, legalities, and emerging trends. Continuous learning will enable you to make informed investment decisions and adjust your strategy as needed.

Conclusion

Starting your journey in real estate investing might seem daunting, but with adequate capital, thorough research, and a solid investment strategy, you'll be well on your way to building a profitable real estate portfolio. Remember, every successful investor started with a single property, learning, and refining their approach along the way. With dedication and due diligence, you too can reap the lucrative rewards offered by real estate investing.

Chapter 4: Types Of Real Estate Investments

Residential Properties

Residential properties are one of the most common real estate investments for beginners due to their familiarity. These encompass:

1. **Single-Family Homes:** These are standalone houses designed for one family or individual. They are the simplest type of residential investment, often rented out for long periods.
2. **Multi-Family Homes:** These are structures designed to house multiple families, with each unit being separate. It provides an opportunity to earn income from multiple tenants.
3. **Vacation Rentals**: These are properties located in vacation hotspots, rented out short-term to tourists. Platforms like Airbnb have made managing vacation rentals more accessible.
4. **Apartment Buildings:** Larger than multi-family homes, apartment buildings can host numerous tenants, often generating substantial rental income.

Investing in residential properties involves understanding the local housing market, tenant rights, and the responsibilities of landlords.

Commercial Properties

Commercial real estate is a broader field, often providing more significant income but requiring more substantial capital and experience.

1. **Office Spaces:** These properties are rented out to businesses and corporations. They often have long-term leases, providing stable income.
2. **Retail Units:** Retail spaces are leased to businesses that

sell goods and services directly to consumers. The landlord may earn a percentage of the tenant's retail sales in addition to the rent.

3. **Shopping Centers and Malls:** Larger than retail units, these host multiple businesses. Rental income is derived from various tenants, making it somewhat resilient to vacancies.
4. **Warehouses and Industrial Spaces:** These are used for manufacturing, storage, or distribution. They usually have longer leases and require less hands-on management.

REITs (Real Estate Investment Trusts)

REITs offer a way to invest in real estate without having to own physical properties, making it an accessible option for many investors.

- **Equity REITs:** The most common type, equity REITs own and operate income-generating real estate. Investors earn through the dividends paid from the income produced by these properties.
- **Mortgage REITs:** These invest in and own property mortgages. Income is generated from the interest earned on these mortgages.
- **Hybrid REITs:** Combining the features of equity and mortgage REITs, hybrid REITs invest in both properties and mortgages.

REITs are typically known for paying high dividends, making them an attractive investment for income-seeking investors.

Real Estate Mutual Funds

Real Estate Mutual Funds invest in securities offered by public real estate companies, including REITs and real estate stocks. These funds aim to provide diversification and liquidity to investors interested in the real estate sector without needing to directly own property. Here are the benefits:

- **Diversification:** Real estate mutual funds invest in a

mixture of equity REITs, mortgage REITs, and other real estate-related securities, providing diversified exposure to the real estate sector.

- **Professional Management:** These funds are managed by experienced professionals who make investment decisions based on thorough analysis and research.
- **Liquidity:** As they are traded on major exchanges, real estate mutual funds can be bought or sold with relative ease, providing liquidity to investors.

Conclusion

The vast landscape of real estate investments offers various opportunities for investors with different financial capabilities, risk tolerance, and investment goals. From direct investments in residential and commercial properties to indirect investments through REITs and real estate mutual funds, there's an option that suits every type of investor. Understanding the distinct features, benefits, and risks associated with each type is crucial for making informed investment decisions and building a successful real estate portfolio.

Chapter 5: Financing Your Real Estate Investment

Mortgage Loans

Mortgage loans are the most common form of financing for real estate investments. Offered by banks, credit unions, and other financial institutions, these loans allow individuals to purchase property by paying a fraction of the total cost upfront (the down payment) and repaying the remainder, with interest, over a specified term.

Types of Mortgage Loans:

- **Fixed-rate Mortgages:** The interest rate remains constant, making monthly payments predictable.
- **Adjustable-rate Mortgages (ARMs):** The interest rate may change periodically, depending on changes in a corresponding financial index.
- **Interest-Only Mortgages**: Initially, you pay only the interest, and later the payments increase, covering both interest and principal.

Requirements: Lenders evaluate credit scores, debt-to-income ratio, employment history, and the value of the property before approving a loan.

Hard Money Loans

Hard money loans are short-term loans provided by private investors or companies. They are often used for investment properties that aren't eligible for traditional financing due to repair needs, the buyer's credit issues, or the quickness with which financing is required.

Characteristics:

- **Short-Term:** Typically 12 months to a few years.
- **High-Interest Rates:** Rates are usually higher than traditional loans.

- **Equity Requirement:** Borrowers must have a significant down payment or equity in the property.
- **Fast Approval:** Loans can be approved and funded quickly.

Hard money loans are often used by house flippers or as bridge loans between the purchase of a new property and the sale of an old one.

Private Money Loans

Private money loans are similar to hard money loans but are sourced from individual private lenders rather than institutions. These are often friends, family, or business associates.

Benefits:

- **Flexible Terms:** Terms can be negotiated and are often more flexible.
- **Quick Access to Funds:** Faster than traditional financing options.
- **Less Stringent Requirements:** Credit scores and income might be less of a concern.

Risks:

- **Legal Compliance:** Both parties must comply with state and federal laws governing such transactions.
- **Relationship Strain:** Mixing business and personal relationships can be risky.

Crowdfunding

Real estate crowdfunding allows multiple investors to pool their money to invest in properties. This method is facilitated through online platforms, making it accessible to many people who wouldn't typically be able to invest in larger real estate deals.

- **Equity Crowdfunding:** Investors acquire small equity shares in a real estate investment. They earn returns based on the rental income and/or the sale of the property.
- **Debt Crowdfunding:** Investors lend money to a real estate developer or project, earning interest on the loan until it's

repaid.

Conclusion

Selecting the right financing option for your real estate investment is crucial and depends on your financial situation, investment goals, and the specifics of the property you intend to purchase. Each financing method comes with its set of requirements, benefits, and risks. Careful consideration and, in some cases, consultation with a financial advisor or lending professional can guide you to make informed decisions that align with your investment strategy and financial plan.

Chapter 6: Selecting The Right Investment Property

Location

The phrase "location, location, location" holds perennial truth in real estate investing. The location of your property can significantly influence its value and rental potential. Here's what you need to consider:

- **Neighborhood Quality:** The safety and desirability of a neighborhood are crucial. Look into crime rates, the quality of local schools, accessibility to public transportation, and proximity to amenities like parks, hospitals, and shopping centers.
- **Market Trends:** Analyze the area's real estate market trends, including property value appreciation and rental yield. Understanding whether it's a buyer's or seller's market will help you make informed investment decisions.
- **Future Development:** Investigate planned developments or zoning changes in the area that might affect property values, positively or negatively.
- **Economic Indicators**: Employment rates, job market growth, and the economic health of the region can impact demand for housing and rental properties.

Property Condition

The state of the property is pivotal, as it affects both the investment cost and the potential rental income.

- **Age:** Older properties may have more character but may also require more maintenance or upgrades.
- **Renovation Needs:** Properties in need of renovation can be acquired at a lower price but consider the cost and time required for improvements.
- **Structural Integrity:** Ensure the property is structurally

sound. Hiring a professional inspector to identify potential issues is often advisable.

- **Energy Efficiency and Sustainability:** Properties with energy-efficient features and sustainable designs may attract more tenants and possibly command higher rents.

Property Value

Understanding the true value of a property is foundational to successful investing.

- **Comparable Market Analysis (CMA):** This involves comparing the property with similar ones that have recently sold in the area to determine its value.
- **Total Investment Cost:** Beyond the purchase price, consider closing costs, renovation expenses, and other fees associated with acquiring and preparing the property for rent or sale.
- **Appreciation Potential:** Look for properties in areas where value is likely to increase over time due to various factors like development projects, improvements in infrastructure, or economic growth.

Rental Income Potential

Your property's ability to generate rental income is a vital aspect of investment success.

- **Rental Yield:** Calculate the annual rental income you can expect against the total cost of the property. The rental yield gives you an indication of the returns on your investment.
- **Occupancy Rates:** Understand the demand for rental properties in the area. High vacancy rates might indicate low demand, which could affect your rental income.
- **Tenant Demographics:** Know your potential tenants. Are they students, families, professionals? This understanding will help in marketing the property effectively.
- **Rent Control Regulations:** Be aware of local laws and regulations regarding rent, as some areas have rent control

policies that might limit the amount you can charge tenants.

Conclusion

Selecting the right investment property requires a confluence of various factors: the location's allure, the property's condition, its inherent value, and potential for generating rental income. It's imperative to approach each factor meticulously, conducting in-depth research and possibly consulting with real estate professionals to guide your decision-making process. Remember, the right property is not just about the physical building but about its financial and locational context, its appeal to tenants, and its potential for growth and income generation in the future. Each property is a significant investment, and as such, each decision should be made with the utmost care and consideration.

Chapter 7: Property Management

Self-management vs Hiring a Property Manager

Owning an investment property comes with numerous responsibilities. As an investor, you'll have to decide whether to manage the property yourself or hire a professional.

Self-management Advantages:

- **Cost Savings:** Avoiding property management fees can increase your profit margin.
- **Direct Control:** Handle issues based on personal judgment without intermediaries.
- **Personal Connection:** Build direct relationships with your tenants, which can lead to better communication and loyalty.

Self-management Disadvantages:

- **Time-Consuming:** Addressing repairs, handling tenant concerns, and overseeing maintenance can be time-intensive.
- **Legal Complexities:** You must familiarize yourself with local landlord-tenant laws.
- **Potential for Mistakes:** Without experience, you might make decisions that aren't in your best financial interest.

Hiring a Property Manager Advantages:

- **Expertise:** Benefit from their experience and industry knowledge.
- **Time Savings:** Let them handle day-to-day operations and tenant concerns.
- **Network Access:** They often have connections with contractors, suppliers, and other professionals.

Hiring a Property Manager Disadvantages:

- **Cost:** Typically charge a percentage of the monthly rental value or a fixed fee.

- **Less Personal Oversight:** Relinquishing direct control might be uncomfortable for some investors.

Duties of a Property Manager

If you decide to hire a property manager, it's essential to understand their role.

- **Tenant Acquisition:** Advertise the property, screen potential tenants, handle lease agreements, and coordinate move-ins.
- **Maintenance and Repairs:** Ensure the property remains in good condition, addressing repairs promptly and overseeing routine maintenance.
- **Rent Collection:** Handle monthly rent collection, managing late payments, and, if necessary, eviction processes.
- **Financial Management**: Provide regular financial reports, manage the property's budget, and potentially pay taxes and mortgages on the investor's behalf.
- **Legal Compliance:** Ensure the property complies with local regulations, including health and safety standards, and manage legal disputes if they arise.

Finding and Managing Tenants

Tenants are the lifeblood of any rental property investment. Finding reliable tenants and maintaining a good relationship with them is vital.

- **Tenant Screening:** It's essential to vet potential tenants by checking their credit history, employment status, rental history, and references.
- **Setting Rent:** Research the local market to set a competitive rent that also meets your ROI goals.
- **Lease Agreements:** A clear lease agreement outlines the rights and responsibilities of both the landlord and tenant, reducing potential conflicts.
- **Tenant Retention:** Keeping reliable tenants is often more

cost-effective than constantly finding new ones. Address their concerns promptly, ensure the property is well-maintained, and consider periodic upgrades to make the property more appealing.

- **Handling Disputes:** Disagreements might arise, be it over repairs, rent, or other issues. Address these diplomatically, and always refer to the lease agreement as a foundational guide.

Conclusion

Property management is a comprehensive task that demands a mix of interpersonal skills, financial savvy, and practical know-how. Whether you choose self-management or hire a professional, understanding the intricacies of property management is crucial to maintaining the value of your investment and ensuring a steady stream of rental income. Proper property management not only sustains your investment but can also enhance its value over time.

Chapter 8: Taxes And Legal Considerations

Understanding Tax Benefits

Real estate investment offers various tax benefits that can significantly increase profitability. Here are some key benefits:

- **Mortgage Interest Deductions:** Interest paid on a mortgage for an investment property is typically deductible against rental income.
- **Depreciation:** While real estate properties often appreciate in value, the IRS allows investors to deduct a portion of the cost of the property (excluding the land) each year, countering the wear and tear.
- **Capital Gains:** When selling a property, the profit (or gain) is subject to capital gains tax. However, if the property was held for more than a year, it's generally taxed at a more favorable long-term capital gains rate.
- **1031 Exchange:** Named after Section 1031 of the U.S. tax code, this allows an investor to sell a property and reinvest the proceeds into a new property while deferring capital gains taxes.
- **Other Deductions:** Various other expenses related to property management, such as property taxes, insurance, and maintenance costs, can be deductible against rental income.

Common Legal Issues

Being aware of potential legal pitfalls can prevent costly disputes and ensure a smoother investment journey.

- **Landlord-Tenant Laws:** Each state has laws that dictate the rights and responsibilities of landlords and tenants. These can cover everything from security deposits to eviction processes.
- **Zoning Laws:** Local zoning laws dictate how a property can

be used. Ensure your intended use for a property aligns with its zoning.

- **Liability Issues:** Property owners can be held liable for accidents that occur on their property. It's essential to maintain a safe environment and consider liability insurance.
- **Contractual Disputes:** Disagreements might arise from misunderstandings or disagreements over lease agreements or property sale contracts.
- **Title Issues:** Ensuring a property's title is clear is crucial. Issues can arise from liens, easements, or other encumbrances.

Working with a Real Estate Attorney

A real estate attorney can be invaluable in navigating the complex world of real estate law.

- **Expertise:** An attorney can provide clarity on intricate legal matters, ensuring you make informed decisions.
- **Contract Review:** They can draft, review, and amend contracts to ensure your interests are protected.
- **Dispute Resolution:** In case of disputes, a real estate attorney can represent your interests, whether in negotiations, mediation, or court.
- **Guidance on Transactions:** They can guide you through the complexities of real estate transactions, ensuring all legal procedures are followed and risks are minimized.
- **Stay Updated:** Real estate laws and regulations change. A real estate attorney can help you stay compliant by updating you on any new changes that may affect your investments.

Conclusion

Understanding the tax benefits associated with real estate investing can dramatically improve profitability. Moreover, awareness of potential legal issues, coupled with the expertise of a real estate attorney, can safeguard your investments and streamline operations. Investing in real estate isn't just about properties and markets; it's also about navigating the intricate web of legal and tax considerations. Proper understanding and guidance in these areas are foundational to a successful real estate investment journey.

Chapter 9: Avoiding Common Mistakes

While real estate investing offers vast opportunities, it also comes with pitfalls that can easily ensnare the unprepared investor. By understanding and avoiding common mistakes, you can mitigate risks and enhance your chances of success.

Lack of Research

Research is the cornerstone of any successful real estate investment.

- **Implications**: Jumping into an investment without adequate research can lead to overpaying for a property, facing unexpected challenges, or missing out on better opportunities.
- **Solution:** Always conduct thorough market analysis. Understand local property values, rental yields, neighborhood safety, and future development plans. Familiarize yourself with local real estate regulations and trends.

Underestimating Expenses

Real estate investing is not without its costs, some of which might not be immediately evident.

- **Implications:** Underestimating expenses can result in negative cash flow, potential debt accumulation, and reduced profit margins.
- **Solution:** Factor in all potential costs, including property taxes, insurance, maintenance, property management fees, and potential vacancy periods. Ensure you have a financial cushion to handle unexpected expenses.

Poor Location Choice

The value and potential of a property are intrinsically tied to its location.

- **Implications:** Investing in a poor location can result in low tenant demand, reduced rental income, and limited property appreciation. The adage "better a bad house in a good location than a good house in a bad location" often holds true in real estate.
- **Solution:** Prioritize location over property features. Look for areas with good amenities, low crime rates, decent infrastructure, and promising future development projects. Research the historical performance of property values and rental yields in the area.

Inadequate Insurance

Protecting your investment is paramount. Insurance safeguards against unforeseen damages and liabilities.

- **Implications:** Without proper insurance, you might face significant financial losses due to property damage, tenant disputes, or liability claims.
- **Solution:** Ensure you have comprehensive property insurance covering potential damages. Consider liability insurance to protect against potential claims from injuries or accidents on your property. Regularly review and update your insurance policies to ensure they remain relevant to your property's value and potential risks.

Conclusion

Mistakes in real estate investing can be costly, both in terms of finances and missed opportunities. However, by being aware of common pitfalls and taking proactive steps to avoid them, you can significantly enhance your chances of building a successful and profitable real estate portfolio. Every challenge offers a learning opportunity, and as you grow and evolve as an investor, these lessons will prove invaluable in steering you towards continued success.

Chapter 10: Building And Growing Your Portfolio

Once you've initiated your journey in real estate investing, the next step is to expand and optimize your portfolio. Building and growing a diverse and robust portfolio requires strategic planning and a keen understanding of the market dynamics.

Diversification

Diversification is a fundamental principle of investing, which reduces risks and potential losses.

Types of Diversification:

- **Geographical:** Investing in properties in different regions or even countries can protect against local market downturns.
- **Asset Type:** Diversify across residential, commercial, industrial, and other property types. Each has its own market dynamics, offering a balance.
- **Investment Type:** Combine direct property ownership with indirect investments like REITs, real estate mutual funds, or crowdfunding.
- **Benefits:** Diversification reduces the impact of any single property or market underperforming, ensuring steady growth and income for your portfolio.

Refinancing and Leveraging

Using the equity built up in properties can provide capital for further investments.

- **Refinancing:** By refinancing a property, you might obtain a better interest rate or tap into the property's increased value, pulling out cash for new investments.
- **Leveraging:** Using borrowed money, especially mortgage loans, allows you to acquire more valuable properties with a smaller upfront investment. This increases potential

returns but also comes with increased risks.

- **Benefits:** Effective refinancing and leveraging strategies can significantly amplify the growth rate of your portfolio. They allow for the acquisition of new properties without heavily depleting your cash reserves.

Scaling Your Investments

Growing a portfolio means moving beyond single investments and looking at the bigger picture.

- **Property Management:** As you acquire more properties, consider hiring property management services or even starting your own property management company.
- **Networking:** Building relationships with other investors, brokers, and industry professionals can open doors to exclusive deals and investment opportunities.
- **Continued Learning:** Stay updated with market trends, emerging investment strategies, and changes in regulations. Consider joining real estate investment clubs or attending seminars.
- **Re-evaluate Strategy:** As your portfolio grows, revisit your investment strategy. Assess the performance of individual assets and the portfolio as a whole. Adjust and optimize based on the current market conditions and future predictions.

Conclusion

Building and growing a real estate portfolio is a continuous journey of learning, adapting, and strategizing. As with any form of investment, there are challenges to face and obstacles to overcome. Yet, with due diligence, a clear strategy, and a passion for the realm of real estate, you can create a portfolio that stands the test of time, bringing both wealth and financial security. Remember, every empire starts with a single foundation stone; your commitment and vision will determine the skyline of your real estate empire.

Conclusion

Summary

"A Beginner's Guide to Real Estate Investing: Passive Income Made Simple" has walked you through the essential aspects of stepping into the real estate investment world. Starting from understanding the basic concepts of real estate and passive income, the guide illuminated pathways to secure initial capital, conduct vital research, and craft an efficient investment strategy. With insights into various types of real estate investments, financing options, and the significance of choosing the right property, the guide also shed light on the nuances of property management, tax benefits, legal considerations, and common mistakes to avoid in the process.

Final Thoughts

Real estate investment is a fascinating and potentially lucrative journey, filled with opportunities and challenges alike. While the prospects of passive income and financial freedom are enticing, success in this field demands dedication, diligence, continuous learning, and strategic planning. Understand that each investment is a learning experience, and every challenge offers valuable insights to refine your strategy and approach. Stay informed, be patient, and maintain a clear vision of your financial goals. With time and effort, real estate investing can indeed become a rewarding venture providing stability, wealth, and financial independence.

Further Reading

For those eager to delve deeper into real estate investing nuances, the following resources can provide additional insights and expertise:

- **"The Book on Rental Property Investing" by Brandon Turner:** Offering actionable advice on building and managing a rental property portfolio.

- **"The Millionaire Real Estate Investor" by Gary Keller:** Provides strategies and wisdom from successful real estate investors.
- **"Real Estate Investing For Dummies" by Eric Tyson and Robert S. Griswold**: A comprehensive guide covering various aspects of real estate investing, suitable for beginners and experienced investors alike.
- **Online Forums and Blogs:** Engage with communities of real estate investors on platforms like BiggerPockets, where experienced investors and newcomers interact, share advice, and discuss industry trends.
- **Real Estate Investment Courses and Seminars:** Consider enrolling in courses offered by reputable institutions or attending seminars conducted by seasoned real estate investors and experts.

Final Word

With the foundational knowledge acquired from this guide, you are now better equipped to embark on your real estate investment journey. Remember, knowledge is power, and informed investing is successful investing. The road ahead may present challenges, but with persistence and a commitment to continuous learning, the destination of financial prosperity is well within reach. Happy investing!

www.ingramcontent.com/pod-product-compliance
Lightning Source LLC
Chambersburg PA
CBHW072226290526
45794CB00007B/2911